FOR THE LOVE OF YOU:
HOW TO NAVIGATE RELATIONSHIPS WITH SPIRITUAL EYES

by Alise Spiritual Healing & Wellness Center

This book may be ordered through booksellers or by contacting:

iGlobal Educational Services, LLC
PO Box 94224 Phoenix, AZ 85070
www.iglobaleducation.com
512-761-5898

Because of the dynamic nature of the Internet, any web addresses or links contained in this book may have changed since publication and may no longer be valid. The views expressed in this work are solely those of the author and do not necessarily reflect the views of the publisher, and the publisher hereby disclaims any responsibility for them.

For the Love of You: *How to Navigate Relationships with Spiritual Eyes*

DEDICATION

This book is dedicated to all individuals who believe in the power of love. Love is the most powerful force on Earth so love yourself enough to attract the right energy that has been destined for you in this lifetime. Without pain, there's no gain. Know that you are not alone and that you are loved, you are valued, and you are competent.

ACKN♡WLEDGMENTS

I cannot say this enough, but I must give glory to God for helping me realize my potential and purpose in life. It was He whom brought Natasa and Dorci together to manifest this project. There are truly no words to express my gratitude as each of you are truly a blessing to our healing center.

I also want to thank Surendra for his creativity in formatting, Pankaj and Umesh for his creativity in designing our book. Each of you are amazing!

CONTENTS

Chapter 1: Before the Relationship 9

The Reasons Why You Should Love Yourself..............................9

Preparing for a Relationship: Your Strategy.................................14

Reflection Questions..16

Importance of coffee talks 17

Importance of quick text-messages 17

The Qualities You Should Look for in a Partner.........................18

How to Move Forward When You Have Been Rejected 20

Chapter 2: The Sweet Beginnings of a Relationship 22

The Love Language: Its Types and Importance 22

The Reasons Why Setting Healthy Boundaries

is Important in a Relationship 25

The Importance of the Date Night 27

Chapter 3: The Metaphysics of Love...30

Karmic Relationships...30

Self-Assessment: Am I in a Past-Life Relationship?...................32

Additional Signs to Look For In Past-Life Connections 33

Self Assessment: What am I learning in this Relatioship? 33

How to Attract the Right Energy for Your Relationship...........35

Positive Affirmations for Honoring Self-Love

for Relationships 35

The Characteristics of Masculine and

Feminine Energy in Relationships...35

Staying in the Divine Order: What It Means...............................37

What Do the Modern-day Proverbs 31 Woman

and Godly Man Look Like?..38

Words of Wisdom From Minister Minister Dr. Alise................40

Chapter 4: The Importance of Intimacy in Relationships........41

Why Having Healthy Discussions about Intimacy is

Healthy in a Relationship 41

Reflection...42

Words of Wisdom from Alise...43

Entertaining Fantasies in a Healthy Way in a Relationship 45

The Benefits of Being in a Supportive Relationship 47

Why Taking Responsibility for Your Part of the

Relationship is Key 49

Chapter 5: Making Progress in a Relationship 52

The Stages of a Relationship...52

The Strategies for Discussing Finances When Dating 55

The Reasons Why Prenuptial Conversations in

Dating Matter 57

Signs to Observe when Dating a Divorced Person 59

The Reasons Why You Should Keep People
Out of Your Business..60
Chapter 6: The Common Categories of
People in a Relationship 63
What Does It Mean to Be Called a Queen or a King?..............63
Why Women Put Men into These Categories:
King, Big Daddy or Handsome 64
Why Men Put Women into Categories such as
Main Chick and Side Chick..66
10 Signs That You Are a Side Chick or a Boo Thang 67
Chapter 7: What We Really Want in a Relationship 69
Men Want Respect; Women Want Love 69
Dating Like a Man: How to Play Hardball..................................71
Chapter 8: Dealing with Conflicts in a Relationship 73
Men Are Intimidated by Strong Women 73
Five Signs That Your Partner Does Not Support
Your Life's Work 74
Dealing with Discovering the New Layers of
the Person That Is Your Partner: Your Strategy 76
Dealing with a Partner Who Uses the Silent Treatment:
What to Do? 77
Dealing with Forgiveness in a Relationship:
How to Move Forward...78
Wisdom from Minister Alise..80

Chapter 9: The Mind Games Men Play in a Relationship.........81

The Mind Games Men Play 81

How to Recognize when a Man Wants to Use You 83

Chapter 10: Approaching the End of the Relationship 86

The Mistakes That Lead to the Loss of Interest

in the Partner 86

Words of Wisdom from Minister Dr. Alise.....................................89

Why You Should Move Forward Without

Closure if the Person Doesn't Share...........................89

How to Walk Away from a Dead or Toxic Relationship 90

Chapter 11: Dealing with a Relationship's End

in a Healthy Way 92

The Questions That Need to Be Answered

after a Breakup..92

How to Deal With a Controlling Ex: Your Place or His............94

The Reasons Why Being Single Is a Good Season in Life 95

Conclusion 97

Where to Go From Here..99

Class Tours and Conferences.................................100

Chapter 1:
BEFORE THE RELATIONSHIP

The start of a relationship is often accompanied by strong excitement. Everything is new, fresh, mysterious, and making those first steps can lead to creating long-lasting memories.

However, the beginning of a romance can also be scary, especially if you're unsure of how to approach it. In order to avoid this kind of stress and make the most out of your time with your wonderful new partner, it is important to prepare before starting a new relationship.

There is a valuable lesson you need to learn before choosing your new partner. It is a very important lesson, perhaps the most important for creating a foundation of a healthy relationship.

Can you guess what it is? Let's take a look at why it is important to love yourself.

The Reasons Why You Should Love Yourself

Perhaps you've heard it said that if you want others to love you, it is important to love yourself first. It is a proven fact that people who feel good about themselves have a way of attracting positive attention from others.

This is probably because you have a way to attract positive energy when others feel the same from you. Simply put, loving yourself will encourage the same vibe from other people. That said, here are a few reasons why you should love yourself:

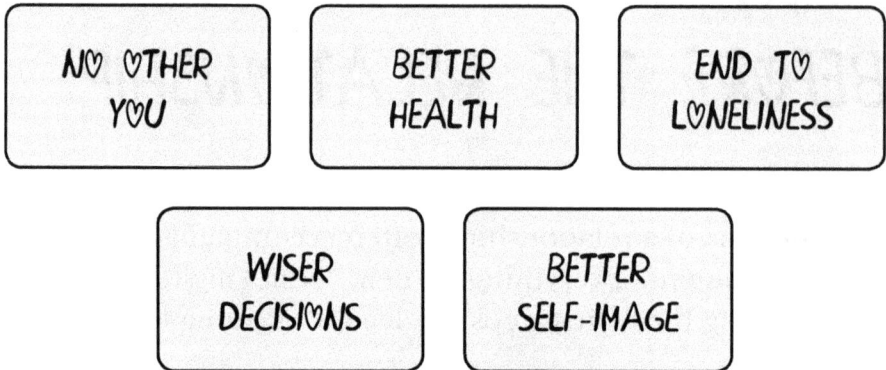

NO OTHER YOU	BETTER HEALTH	END TO LONELINESS

WISER DECISIONS	BETTER SELF-IMAGE

There is no other you in the entire world ever.

Do you know how unique you are? Think about it: There is no one like you anywhere in the world. No one has the combination of characteristics that make up who you are.

Take a moment to realize how valuable you are by knowing that there is no one quite like you on the entire planet. Once you realize this, you will see how important it is to fall in love with yourself.

Let's look at a few of our client's stories regarding how they dealt with this in their life.

Scenario: "I'm Through With It"

Clint invited to cover his friend, Chloe's hotel expenses while she visited his city. Things were going smoothly since Clint picked Chloe up from the airport as he promised. Chloe though that Clint would take care of her transportation needs for that week, but she quickly learned that he was using someone else's car and could not deliver. He did pay for the first two nights of her five day stay before heading to Florida for a business conference. When it came time to pay for the third night, Clint could not deliver. This left Chloe very upset, but she forgave him and carried on as if nothing happened. The very next day, he took her to a local coffee shop and they had a little coffee talk that turned into an argument over money. Chloe didn't want to press the issue because she needed him to go with her for business. Three days later, they are in Florida and it came time for the business presentation. Clint started the presentation and went mute. They could not complete the presentation, which shocked Chloe. When it came time to leave Florida, Clint had promised that he would cover the plane tickets. Chloe learned that he didn't deliver once again. She purchased her plane ticket and got the hell out of dodge without HIM! She later learned that he had four other women who he was using for money. A month later, Chloe reached out to Clint only to learn that he would not answer. It took Chloe some time to get over this three-year friendship but she eventually came to terms. Three months later, Chloe met a new friend named, Jackson Mayweather, a millionaire, who owned several businesses.

Wisdom from Minister Dr. Alise

In Chloe's case, I am glad that she found out the truth about Clint. Plain and Simple, he could not provide and he was not ready for such a connection. It is important for Chloe to recognize the type of connection that they had and the plethora of lessons in which they taught each other. I pray that they both learned the lessons so that they can move on to a new level of learning. It seems that Chloe upgraded, but just because a man is a millionaire doesn't mean that all problems are solved. There will still be life lessons that will need to be taught and learned. After all, Earth is a huge university. The biggest take-a-way is even when other people leave your life, you will be able to pick yourself up when you know the truth of the matter. Honor yourself and keep moving forward.

Loving yourself brings you better health.

Love makes people more caring, and this includes the people who love themselves. Most of the time, this involves taking good care of yourself and includes not only your emotional well-being, but your physical health as well.

The moment you attain self-love you will be more mindful of your diet, and this, in turn, affects your general well-being. You will also take the time to work out so as to maintain a healthy body.

Loving yourself means an end to loneliness.

When you love yourself, you never lack for company. This is because you are your own friend and have no problem engaging in activities on your own. When you enjoy your own company, you will be capable of being a good friend to others. And even if other people leave your life, you will be able to pick yourself up by doing what you like.

Loving yourself leads to wiser decisions.

Have you seen some people make irrational decisions regarding their life? These often lead to disasters, and you are left wondering what prompted them to do that.

Self-love lets you make the right choices regarding your life. It serves as a measuring scale which enables you to weigh your options and make the best decisions.

Loving yourself leads to a better self-image.

Through the eyes of love, you are a better person to yourself. Confidence stems from loving yourself just the way you are.

Scenario: "Part-Time is Not My Destiny"

William, a successful business, met a young serial entrepreneur, at a networking event on the West Coast. He was very attracted to her beauty, but whom he heard her speak on Domestic Abuse she fell in love. Immediately, after her presentation, he asked to book an appointment with her, but she declined. After taking his business card, she googled him to find out that he was well accomplished as well. Being the curious and courageous woman that one is known for, she invited him to lunch. One business lunch turned into five lunches and several conversations later. Grace felt comfortable being his friend on social media only to learn that he was very married. Grace thought that she could handle it, but William had mastered the art of pervasion. They both got caught up in the moment and ended up in bed together. They had passionate, hot sex every other day and that continued for well over 3 months. Grace had never done such and everywhere she turned her heart was convicted. She woke up one day only to discover that she had missed her period. She carried a heavy burden around until one built up the courage to book a doc's appt. It was a tanta-lizing week before she got her blood test results back. It turns out that she was not pregnant. At that time, Grace promised herself that she had to do better. While she would miss the sex, she felt like she gained so much more - her dignity. Grace broke the news to William and he was not happy but she was sure that he would find someone else. After all, she wasn't the first and probably wouldn't be the last woman to fall victim to his system.

Words of Wisdom from Minister Dr. Alise

Grace did the right thing by breaking it off with William. Nobody is perfect, but this lesson was more for her so that she could value herself and feel good about her decisions by setting that healthy boundary.

When it comes to William, there are several emotional issues going on and it may be that there is a true emotional connection with his wife. For one reason or another, they have broken down in that area. William has to resolve these issues on his own. Grave or his wife cannot fell that void. When William is ready, God will be there for him to help make the decisions that will honor his Truth. Will has the power within to make this change. Remember, you are loved, valued and competent.

Preparing for a Relationship: Your Strategy

Some strategies are needed in order to create and maintain a relationship. When you consider going into a relationship, certain things have to be in place so that it can prosper. Mainly this has to do with each partner working at being a better person. So, how do you go about doing this? Let's take a look at these five strategies:

OPEN	POSITIVE	REASSURANCE

COMMON FRIENDS	SHARE CHORES

Be open with your feelings

You will become a better partner if you don't hold back on the way you feel. It is easier to communicate when you are willing to speak out to the person you're starting a relationship with. You should learn to talk to your partner in an efficient manner so that no misconceptions occur between you two.

Scenario: "You Plan Last Minute and I Plan Ahead"

Jacob, a businessman, had been dating Shelly, an entrepreneur, for almost six months. When she met Jacob, business was good and he was able to maintain the life style that comes with being an in-demand leader. During month 5, Shelly decided it was time for her to share some of her finances with him. After sharing a picture of $250 in cash with him on social media, he waited three days to ask for money. He told her that she would pay her back and one agreed to it. Things were going good and she even supported him by attending his professional event. Two weeks passed, Jacob asked for another $60 for a print job. At that point, Shelly was apprehensive about helping him, but one did it anyway. As Shelly was driving to the ATM, Jacob texted her and started being controlling with his words. By the time she gets the money out of the bank, Jacob had managed to change the location of where they were going to go over business plans. Shelly and Jacob hardly ever argue, but this time Shelly opened up and told Jacob how she really felt and she lift him. He begged her not to leave, but she did anyway because she was tired of his demanding ways. Jacob cut off communication for two weeks leaving Shelly feeling empowered and confused at the same time.

Reflection Questions

1. What could Jacob have done differently?
   _____
   _____
   _____

2. Do you think Shelly made the right decision? Why or Why not?
   _____
   _____
   _____

3. What advice would you offer this couple during this phase of the relationship?
   _____
   _____
   _____

Be positive

People who are positive tend to infect others with it. It is more so in a marriage, where partners relate on a more personal level. With a positive attitude, you are more likely to be encouraging to your partner than otherwise. Relationships thrive on uplifting one other, and it can be by way of words or attitude.

Below are some ways that you can be positive and supportive with your partner:

1. Send daily inspirational quotes.
2. Quick test messages of specific positive affirmations.
3. Leave sweet post-it notes around the house, in their lunch, or even work space.
4. Create intimate poems that will touch their Heart.

If you are looking for examples, then below are some examples:

1. Inspirational Quote
2. Positive Affirmation Example
3. Intimate Poem

Reassure each other

Couples should declare the will to remain together over time. It works to establish commitment in each of them so that they both know they are together in the long haul. Be a reassuring partner so you can work towards a common goal, thus being better able to share the responsibilities in ensuring the success of your relationship. Your partner should be aware he/she can depend on you.

Importance of coffee talks

Communication can be challenge when both partners are busy. One strategy to use to promote communication beyond the bedroom and this can be done over a coffee talk. If you don't like coffee, then change it to a tea talk. Just make sure you are not talking over alcoholic drinks.

Importance of quick text-messages

A quick text-message or chat can go along way with your partner. You can send messages that focuses on your partner or even yourself. Your partner will love it, but you have to send these when your heart tells you. You don't want to over send these messages as they will become expected. You want your partner to appreciate the little things that matter.

For both of these strategies, it is important to also express your gratitude and empower your partner. Now, that's sexy!

Have common friends

Having common friends makes a couple more grounded in a relationship. The kind of friends you keep has a direct influence on who you are. When you share your friends with your partner, you have the support of people you both know, and you share the good and bad times with them.

Share your chores

Do not set aside certain tasks for one of you, instead be ready to share them between the two of you. This way, the feeling of being in a partnership gets enhanced.

The Qualities You Should Look for in a Partner

Different people look for different things in a partner. While some look for specific physical attributes of a person whom they are interested in forming a relationship with, others differ in priorities.

However, in as much as preferences differ, some common ones appear across the range of people in search of a partner. Here is a breakdown of a few of them:

Trust

You know the feeling of having confidence in the one you are dating. Nothing beats knowing you can bank on the one closest to you. Trust is the single most important quality to look for in a partner. Many have lost meaningful relationships after a breach of trust to another. Trust comes from a decision to be honest with each other at all times.

Reliability

It is important for partners in a relationship to support each other. The primary need of anyone seeking a partner is having their emotional needs met within the relationship. You will want to know you have the backing from the one closest to you. For that to happen, each of you has to be reliable in offering support to the other.

Chemistry

Between you and the one you are interested in there should be chemistry going on. An attraction to each other will keep the sparks flying between the two of you, therefore, be sure you have that going on. Not only that, but you also need to ensure you keep those feelings alive by fanning them as time goes by.

Openness

Have you ever witnessed two people who genuinely love one another on a constant war path with each other? Most likely you will find that either one or both of them are not open to the other. A relationship requires that both involved be open with each other as a basis for understanding. It is what makes for trust to build up between the two.

Maturity

Look for a partner that is mature enough to nurture you emotionally. You will find it difficult to get along with one who does not own up to his shortcomings. Maturity entails being responsible for one's actions at all times. Knowing what is expected of you and then going ahead to do it is a character of a mature person. It comes with a level of responsibility allowing you to admit when you are wrong.

One thing you need to keep in mind is that good relationships take effort from those involved. It will be worth your while to put in some for yours to work.

But there is one last thing you need to consider before approaching the person you want to start a relationship with, and this is the possibility of being rejected.

How to Move Forward When You Have Been Rejected

In different areas of life, people face rejection and are unable to deal with it the right way. Being denied something you want can be a painful experience that leaves many unable to move on with life after that.

A series of reactions follow when you get rejected by another whom you consider important. At first, you do not want to believe it has happened to you, and then when it starts to sink in, you can react in various ways.

It might seem as if a certain light has gone off in your life, and you fall into despair and gloom. One of the top things rejection robs a person of is the feeling of security in having the other person in their life.

There are some things that could help you move on after being rejected, but a lot depends on the way you respond to it. Here are some ways to help you move on after being rejected.

Admit you are hurting from the experience and then forge ahead after that.

Denying the disappointment and hurt that rejection causes won't help you in any way. It is much like burying your head in the sand, and yet you will have to face up to reality sooner or later.

Be kind on yourself and do not beat yourself up.

Quit blaming yourself for what happened, and instead think positively.

Do not let rejection change the way you view yourself. Just because that one person thinks you are not worth their time does not mean it is the end of dating for you. The best you can do is to move on with the hope you will find another who is worth your while.

Take a lesson from it.

There is always something you can learn from any experience in life and rejection is one of them. Take a good look at any way you might have contributed to it, and work on improving in that area. You will realize it may not be such a bad thing after all as you become a better person from it.

By following the advice presented to you in this chapter, you will be able to enter a new relationship confidently, and still enjoy the exciting new feelings it brings. Congratulations! In the next chapter, we will take a look at some of the things that follow the start of a great relationship.

♡

Chapter 2:
THE SWEET BEGINNINGS OF A RELATIONSHIP

In the first chapter, we outlined some things you need to know before making the big step of starting a new relationship. But what happens after that first step is equally as important, as love needs not only a great foundation, but also strong material for it to grow.

Being in love is very much like planting a flower: it needs nurture and care in order to bloom. For that reason, let's take a look at some of the things that mark the start of a loving relationship.

The Love Language: Its Types and Importance

Now that you have found love it is time to find ways to continue expressing it to your partner. There are various ways of doing it and the main purpose of all of them is expressing your emotions to your better half. What are some of the ways you can use to communicate love to your partner? Here's a look at some of them:

Spend time together.

Like most relationships, love requires that the two involved spend time together. It's not enough just to be there physically, it has to be quality time during which each of you gives undivided attention to the other. Taking a walk down a lonely path together or going out for a meal are just some of the ways you can spend time together. Depending on where you live, you can also enjoy the sunrises and sunsets. Each community has places that you can spend time together and make it your own special hiding place, just for the two of you.

Give gifts to each other.

You know that special feeling when someone gives you something meant just for you. Exchange of gifts between two people who love each other reveals the special nature of their relationship as it shows that they give attention to each other and keep one another in their thoughts. Giving is a big part of showing you care for one another, and should be given preference in a relationship. Remember, it's not about the money as the focus should be on gifts that don't cost a dime.

The importance of a touch

Physical touch ranks top among the best ways for one to show emotion, and this is especially noticeable in a romantic relationship. It is important to know what works best for your partner, what gives him or her the most pleasure. Some are fine simply holding hands while others desire a more intimate feel of the partner. Whatever the case, be sure to discover what works for your partner so you can engage in it more often. You may want to ask for permission because you don't know if touch is something that the partner can handle. For example, imagine meeting your partner for coffee and having a genuine conversation. While your partner is talking, gently hold his or her hand and see how he or she responds to it.

Do a service to one other.

One sure way to please your partner is for you to do things for them. Find out what he or she likes having done for them, and then, by all means, do it. Simple acts of kindness go a long way in communicating love between partners. It might only be taking out the trash while your partner fixes dinner, but the simple act goes a long way in showing how much you care for the other. If you are in the dating phase, then you should ask these questions.

Below are some questions to help you find out what you need to know:

Questions To Ask While Dating

1. What do you like to do for fun? How does that look?
2. What is your love language towards serving your partner?
3. What do you want from me? Why?
4. What do you think that I want from you? Why?
5. How important is communication to you?

Give compliments to each other.

Nothing is as important in a relationship as giving compliments to each other. It is a sure way for partners to appreciate each other. As humans, we are born with an innate need to be appreciated, something you should not limit when it comes to your partner. Go on, be generous with those kind words and enhance your love for each other. When you are giving compliments, you want it to be genuine. If you can help it, focus on compliments outside of the work in which they do. It needs to be an emotional connection.

Expressing love is important, but so is having clear and healthy boundaries when it comes to your relationship. Let's take a look at why that is so:

The Reasons Why Setting Healthy Boundaries Is Important in a Relationship

Boundaries are important in any relationship as they spell how far those in it can go when dealing with one another. Much like the ones established to separate states, those boundaries determine how far one can go without going too far into the space of the other.

It is important to note that, even in the most loving of relationships, there's need for those involved to have personal space. So, what are the reasons why healthy boundaries matter in a relationship? Here are a few insights on the issue:

Clarity of needs

It is one thing to have needs that are only known to you, and another to let your partner in on them. To avoid misunderstandings, you need to spell out your likes, as well as those things with which you are not quite comfortable. This reduces misunderstandings between you two, as you are both be in tune with each other's needs. One suggestion is to have those conversations over coffee/tea so that it is in a conversational environment and not in the bedroom. You want your bedroom to be associated with peace, passion, emotional intimacy. The bottom line is to make sure that you provide a confirmation after your partner has met one or more of your needs. If you are not able to say it to them verbally, then leave a nice note for them to read. Again, this depends on the love language between the two of you.

Ease of Communication

When both partners in a relationship have clear boundaries in place, they promote better communication between them. It is easier expressing your feelings with the knowledge of how far you can go with each other. Should anything happen within the relationship, the partners are comfortable to speak on it.

CAUTION:

If you try to bring up something and your partner is not ready to talk about it, then don't force it. Keep a journal and reflect upon the situation. This will allow you to emotionally process the situation so that you are prepared to listen when the time comes to discuss with your partner.

Nurture Respect Between Partners

Respect is necessary for a relationship. Knowledge of what works for your partner will help you steer off stepping on their toes. This could be one of the leading causes of conflict between you two. It becomes easy for respect to exist when healthy boundaries are in place.

Tip:

This takes a lot of coffee talks and a lot of listening. It is important to get to know your partner outside of the bedroom. This will allow you to understand where your partner is coming from, when conflicts arise. In other words, it gives you an opportunity to learn how to resolve conflicts before they even get started.

Promote Growth and Commitment

Relationships flourish when those involved are comfortable in each other's company. One way for this to happen is for you two to be on the same page on your preferences. Open lines of communication stimulate growth in a relationship, which in turn leads to the closer commitment between you.

Offer a Boost to Confidence of Those Involved

It is important for those in a relationship to be confident in their support of each other. For instance, two people involved in a romantic relationship can attain closer intimacy through having confidence in each other.

Having firm boundaries will go a long way to help this, and in turn, it will create a situation where the two are comfortable and gain acceptance of each other.

It is vital that people in a relationship feel accepted in order to be able to nurture openness with each other. With healthy boundaries in place, this should be no trouble to achieve.

Once you're comfortable in your new relationship, don't forget to keep having fun! Let's look at why going on dates help with keeping your relationship exciting and fresh.

The Importance of the Date Night

The importance of date night cannot be overruled in a relationship. For these occasions, you two get the chance to dress up and make up for your date together.

Time spent by the two of you on a date enhances communication while also serving as a way to release stress. Away from the kids or distractions in the home, you two are then able to focus on your relationship.

As a couple, you should plan on constantly going on a date every so often. Here are just some of the reasons why the date night is valuable:

Communication

Communication is imperative for a close relationship. Going out on a date night allows the two of you to take on issues relating to you both. Through such communication on a regular basis, you will be able to keep in touch with each other's life.

Freshness

Away from the familiar territory where things are taken for granted, having fun together in a new setting can be especially interesting. You can take part in activities that interest you both, and by doing so strengthen your intimacy.

Stress Relief

Get rid of stress by tugging your partner along for a date night. Through emotional support and intimate conversation that takes place when you regularly go out with him or her, you will bring down each other's stress levels.

Bringing the Spark Back

It is easy for a couple to lose the spark that brought them together, but you can reignite it when you go out on a date night together. That way, the date night works to sustain your love over time.

Stronger Attachment

Out on a date night, you are more likely to feel more attached to your partner. This leads to the deeper commitment between the two of you, resulting in a more satisfying bond.

You are making progress towards turning your relationship into something stable and secure: the very beginning of a true love. In the next chapter, we will take a look at some of the spiritual aspects of the bond that forms between the two people in love.

Chapter 3:
THE METAPHYSICS OF LOVE

ove is not something that follows every relationship. It can, however, be found when two people create a firm basis for it to grow, feeding it with care and intimacy. Then, it evolves into something more than the physical; it transcends onto another plane of existence.

This is why it's such an elusive topic in both philosophy and poetry: love is so vast and indescribable, and yet it's such an important aspect of our lives as humans. In this chapter, we will take a look at some of the spiritual views on love and relationships.

Karmic Relationships

It is well known that actions have got effects when karma is in play. In a Karmic relationship, a connection takes place between two people that might even barely know each other.

A single encounter might succeed in establishing the feeling of familiarity with another. It is as if the two know each other from someplace unknown to either of them.

Most life relationships are karmic, as it involves a connection with another person. It is karma that is responsible for bringing people together. That includes family, as one does not choose where they are born.

Soul mates

A soul mate is a person with whom you get drawn into a relationship. There is no logical way to explain how it happens, as you feel compelled to be together. A soul mate brings out the best in you, yet you have no way to explain how the two of you came together.

Take lovers, for instance. You meet a person, and get a strong urge to be together. This has to do with the soul being able to let you know you should get in a relationship with the other. Attraction might play a part in it, but the effects of karma bind you to the one you are meant to be with.

It does not guarantee you will be together forever, though. This kind of love has great potential, but it is often riddled with plenty of obstacles for most people.

Twin flames

You might come across a person that feels quite familiar, as if you have met before. Even though you know for certain you have not met before, it is as if you know each other from somewhere.

Telepathy has a lot to do with twin flames, as you are both able to pick up each other's vibe. You share similar thoughts with the person, as you do feelings, even when miles apart.

The soul is the window of one's heart, and so, if the two meet and look into each other's eyes, it can feel as if staring into each other's soul. A sign that you have met your twin flame is the intense feeling of love and affection when thinking about a person you have only just met.

You may feel complete now that you are together at last. One thing is for sure: both of you know you were meant to be together. It feels as if you finally found the person you have long been looking for.

Past Life Connections

Love at first sight! Wrong! In a past-life connection, it can feel as if that person is your soulmate because you have overwhelming emotions and a sense of recognition. After talking to each other, you may begin to understand that the two of you share a great deal of life experiences that only bring you two closer together emotionally.

The purpose of past-life relationships is to make you take a deep look at your relationship with you. Past-life relationships are full of lessons and you must learn the lessons to be able to move forward in a better relationship that honors the real you. These types of relationships are plagued with many problems and a range of emotions that can be addictive. Individuals may even report spiritual experiences such as telepathy, visions, and seeing colors during love-making.

Here's a Self-Assessment to help you:

Self-Assessment: Am I in a Past-Life Relationship?

1. Can I sleep at night about this relationship?

_____

_____

_____

2. Is this relationship making us better people?

_____

_____

_____

3. Has this relationship strengthen my faith and values?

_____

_____

_____

If you answered, yes, this may be a soulmate connection.

If you answered, no, then it is a past-life connection and you got to let it go to set yourself free.

That's the first self-assessment that you need to ask yourself, but you also need to continue looking out for these signs as you get to know the person more.

Additional Signs to Look For In Past-Life Connections

Before we go any further, let's look at five questions that will help you determine if you are experiencing a past-life connection. These questions are the following:

Self Assessment: What am I learning in this Relatioship?

1. What did he or she teach you about yourself?

_____

_____

_____

2. What recurring patterns are you noticing?

_____

_____

_____

3. How is this person helping you? Is it for no apparent reason?

_____

_____

_____

4. Do you owe them anything after the relationship is over?

_____

_____

_____

5. Do you have anything left over after the relationship is over?

_____

_____

_____

You may find yourself getting involved with this partner's day-to-day life. Before this occurs, it is important to pay attention to your intentions, as well as his or her. At some point, one or both of you will end up doing things that cannot be returned after the relationship is over. For instance, if the relationship does not work out, then the partner may leave a child, book, animal, knowledge, money, or whatever is deemed sentimental with you. If you (or that individual) owe you something, don't expect to get it back. In other words, whatever he or she has left you with is there to stay with you and there's nothing you can do about it. In the same token, whatever he or she owes you, don't expect to get it. The same is true if you left or owe this person something. What's done is done and it is part of their connection to you. At face value, you may look at this as a bad thing, but in reality, your past-life connections are extremely important to you as they help you learn and grow more spiritually.

How to Attract the Right Energy for Your Relationship

The ultimate challenge in past-life relationships is to learn to let go of that type of energy so that you can attract the right energy that is meant for you because you are worthy. The law of attraction is very important so you want to make sure that you are sending out the right type of vibration and be more conscious of what you are trying to manifest.

Below are a few positive affirmations to help you begin to attract true love and a relationship that has your best interest at heart. They are the following:

Positive Affirmations for Honoring Self-Love for Relationships

1. I am worthy of a relationship that is worthy of me.
2. I deserve a relationship that nurtures me.
3. I deserve a relationship that is equal in body, mind, and spirit.
4. I deserve a relationship that doesn't destroy my heart.
5. I deserve a relationship that does not take away from my self-esteem.

Now, let's focus on masculine and feminine energy and how it works in a relationship.

The Characteristics of Masculine and Feminine Energy in Relationships

Relationships that have sexual attraction and a strong intimate connection have opposite energies in action. You can have deep physical chemistry with others that possess a different energy to the one you have most of the time.

Every person has variable degrees of the two energies, even though there is one naturally dominant in each of us. It is, however, wrong to associate female and male energies with corresponding genders. It is important to understand that masculine energy is born out of challenge and repetition while feminine energy is created by praise.

There's a distinct difference between the way masculine energy and feminine energy get expressed. Lack of understanding of the two creative energies might lead to an imbalance in a relationship between you and your partner.

It is evident that feminine and masculine types of energies lead to different ways of communication. A look at the differences between the two might offer useful insight on the issue.

Masculine energy consists of angles and straight lines. On the other hand, feminine energy is made of swirls and curves. Regarding speed, masculine energy is dull and slow, while feminine energy is fast and energized. To be exact, whereas feminine energy has 140 points of energy masculine energy has 40 points of energy. This makes quite a big difference between the two.

Some of the characteristics of feminine energy are those of being fluid, very creative and very broad. This makes it possible to do several things simultaneously, taking advantage of the curves and swirls. You get the point, right?

Masculine energy is directed on a straight line and will go from A to B then to C and back again to the beginning. The two energies are essential for a balance in creation. Without feminine energy, masculine energy is incomplete, lacking in value, not appreciated, and nurtured. One's personal balance are thus incomplete. Feminine energy without masculine energy is unsupported, incomplete, and unfocused, as well as, scattered, and unbalanced. Without purpose, it lacks a sense of success.

When this energy is unbalanced, a man may cheat looking for support or a woman may feel suppressed because the man is aggressive. It is important to understand that any partner who decides to cheat is his or her own free will. However, it is important to recognize that the underlying issue in these situations are both emotional and energetic imbalances. Therefore, it is important for individuals to select relationships that radiate at the same spiritual energy as that is what being yoked means in the sacred Bible. It has nothing to do with finances, but everything to do spiritually and emotionally as you become one in body, mind, and spirit.

Staying in the Divine Order: What It Means

The divine order stipulates that there is a place and order of importance in the spiritual nature of things. The power of a person is determined by the more 'spirit' he or she has. This explains the hierarchy of the authority of living organisms as opposed to non-living objects such as rocks.

Staying in the divine order means that you accept the way things are at any moment in your life and that everything happens for good in life. It doesn't matter what might be going on, but you believe it is meant to be, and take rest in the knowledge. You accept that the way certain people are is exactly the way they are supposed to be at the moment. Your life is going as it is destined to and you are fine with it, and you find peace living in divine order.

Human beings have a connection to a higher being which serves as the spiritual source. Knowledge of this and the divine ability of the source to give us what we need to go through life at the time we need it gives us rest. Anything that goes wrong in life is as a result of going against the flow that has a positive influence on us. Otherwise, we are meant to allow the power to steer us through life.

At times our deep-rooted belief in the difficulty of life makes it difficult for us to trust. We need only affirm Divine Order when things appear to go wrong in life through remaining in the active flow. Trust comprises an important part regarding this attitude. Divine order is about staying in the positive flow of life. We affirm it when life does not go as it should and relax into the truth thereof.

We thus rest in the knowledge that things are going exactly the way they are meant to go. It doesn't matter the delays or challenges as we believe all happens for the good of us. Finding peace in all that might be going on in life allows us to relax in whatever situation in life. This way we stay clear of negative emotions and get empowered in the process. We enjoy life more by allowing the flow of life to carry us through. When it comes to divine order in one's lives, then it is important to approach life in this order: 1) Spirit; 2) Spouse; 3) Family; and 4) Everything else.

What Do the Modern-day Proverbs 31 Woman and Godly Man Look Like?

The Bible talks of the virtues suitable for a godly woman in Proverbs 31. Many aspire to be this kind of a woman but find it difficult in the modern day. It might seem like a lot is required of one such, to the extent that it feels impossible to fulfill the role. It is, however, possible for one who seeks strength from God as it is the only way to live lives that are worthy of him.

A Proverbs 31 Woman and Godly Man have several characteristics in common with one another. They include:

Hard work. Neither of them courts laziness but have their hands full working for their households. Nothing is out of reach as they do all they can, getting up early to start off work.

Kindness embodied in the lives of these two who do not hesitate to be a blessing to those around them. The poor and needy have a place in their lives as they welcome them with open arms.

They **have good character** and **cherish righteousness** in all that they do. Walking in dignity and wisdom, they project the image of virtue wherever they are.

The fear of God is part of their lives and can be seen by those close to them.

With all that life has going on a man or woman should live their lives according to the statutes set for them by God. They should be the light of the world and in the view of others a representation of the love of God. Merely by the way they lead their lives they should minister to others in the way they carry themselves.

Hard work and character are never far away from the two that are the model of modern day Christianity. Striving to do right and not relegate on the duties set before them, the modern-day Proverbs 31 Woman and Godly Man represent the real image of Christ today. You should imitate these two as they provide examples of the way life should be for those who bear the name of Christians.

Words of Wisdom From Minister Minister Dr. Alise

As a Minister and Intuitive Life Coach, I see a great deal of clients regarding love and relationships. Men want a virtuous woman, but they don't know how to put out the right kind of energy to attract, needless to say, keep such a woman. Virtuous women require support on all levels, including financially, physically, emotionally, and spiritually. This is where men have to take a step back and focus on their partner's needs and release the ego. Leadership can be shown without all the bull. Aggression and control should not be the type of energy utilized in such a connection as they are not fruits of the Spirit.

When it comes to women, I see that they strive to be a virtuous woman, but they don't know how to tap into their own personal power. Typically, they give their power away to others and are not able to set those healthy boundaries. Until that is fixed, this will be an ongoing challenge that will impact both partners and their relationship.

Chapter 4:
THE IMPORTANCE OF INTIMACY IN RELATIONSHIPS

ntimacy consists of feelings of oneness in emotional love and connection with each other. You long to share your deepest thoughts with the other as well as feelings that exist between the two of you. There needs to be a required level of caring, acceptance, and trust for such a relationship to prosper.

Why Having Healthy Discussions about Intimacy is Healthy in a Relationship

There are different intimacy relationships and knowing what works for you as a couple helps safeguard your relationship. Here are some of them:

Physical Intimacy

This is a huge lure when getting involved with another person. Let your partner know your preferences in the physical so you can explore them together. Assuming that the other person knows what works for you is wrong as this may not be the case.

Scenario: "Don't Assume... .Just Ask!"

William and Bella had been dating for five months. When they first connected, their conversations lasted hours and hours but they never discussed sex. One particular day, they made a mutual decision to meet outside of their regular meeting place for coffee. This time, they decided to meet at Bella's house. Things progressed from talking to kissing and the next thing they knew they were both naked in bed. William and Bella had sex for the first time only to later find out that William criticized her for not being able to perform the woman-on-top position as he had desired. Immediately, Bella became distant and cut-off communication from him. Two days later, Bella posted her anniversary of being able to walk and care for herself after flirting with the idea of being paralyzed from a car wreck that she didn't even cause. William had no clue that Bella had a very bad car wreck that left her for dead. He found out about it on Facebook, but this was after he had told her that she needed "fuck school". It was too late because the damage had been done.

Reflection

1. If you were in Bella's situation, what would you have done?

   _____

   _____

   _____

2. Do you think that Bella made the right decision for herself? Why or why not?

_____

_____

_____

3. What advice would you give William?

_____

_____

_____

4. What advice would you give Bella?

_____

_____

_____

Words of Wisdom from Alise

Physical intimacy is so complex, but it doesn't have to be if partners communicate. Shame on Will! It is important to understand that physical intimacy in a relationship is about 10% and it should not be a deal-breaker. Bella had every right to pull away and focus back on herself. Just like there was a lesson for William, you can rest assure that Bella learned something from this relationship experience as well. The morale of this story is to don't be too quick to judge others as you don't know the flow of their heart or their story.

Recreational Intimacy

It comes about from spending time together with others with similar interests. Couples need to have this with each other or others outside the relationship to maintain their individual identity of each. Between a couple, it ends up making the time spent together well worth the time as you both engage in casual fun.

Aesthetic Intimacy

It is about having shared interests with your partner. When you discover that you share similar likes for some things or live with the choice of the other, despite being different from yours, both of you are thus aesthetically compatible. Most often, it requires knowledge about the likes of each of you in the relationship.

Love Tip:

This is a good way to have topics to discuss during coffee talks.

Emotional Intimacy

Both of you are secure in being yourselves in the relationship with emotional intimacy. You can let yourself expose your weaknesses to your partner, secure in the knowledge of not being judged. Much as many desire this kind of intimacy, only a few couples can attain it.

Scenario: "I Thought You Said... You Heard Me Say WHAT?"

James and Monica has been dating for eight months. Lately, James had been under pressure at work and Monica was dealing with her own issues. Her period was late and she was worried that she might be pregnant. Monica communicated this to James and he started crying. James pulled away for two weeks. He later resurfaced with an apology. He told her that he only heard, "I AM PREGNANT". Monica made sure that she said that her words did not come out right and James started crying again. She didn't say anything because she didn't want to go back instead of moving forward. Both James and Monica are still in the relationship after this miscommunication.

This is just an example of how emotional intimacy can help a couple work through their issues.

Sexual Intimacy

Attained when two people in a relationship are comfortable in their nakedness. You have no qualms about being seen by your partner in the full glare of lights and share dreams and preferences regarding sex. Secure in your spouse's company, too. Discuss with your partner about the various kinds of intimacy that work best for each of you.

Love Tip:

You may not be comfortable at first, but try to get creative and spend a great deal of time discussing the matter in a playful way.

Entertaining Fantasies in a Healthy Way in a Relationship

For a relationship to be healthy, the spark that drove two people together should continue to glow as the time passes. Initially, when two people meet, they are often unable to keep their hands off each other due to the emotions coursing through them. With time, they begin to fade and need fanning to keep them alive. You can find some ways to do just that below:

Shared Fantasies

Did you know that sharing sexual fantasies with your partner can be a turn on for them? Listening to the things that make your partner go gooey can have such a stimulating effect on you two. It happens when the two of you are relaxed, away from other responsibilities. So, take time over the weekend to live out each others' fantasies for a fun-filled time together that will leave the embers coming alive some more.

Each Sex Life is Different

Some people like to talk about their intimate moments with others outside the relationship. Be wary of doing so as couples vary and sexual patterns are not the same. Trying a roll in the hay every other day like the couple across the street will only leave you exhausted. After all, who knows how true their assertions are?

CAUTION:

This is how you get your man or woman taken or borrowed. Keep your relationship to yourself, especially your sex life.

Slot in Time to Have Sex

Despite the speed of modern life, there is no reason for any couple to neglect the role of sex. Take a chance to explore your fantasies as a pair by setting aside a time every so often. Going by your preference as a couple, agree on the number of occasions for you to have sex each week and stick to it. This is a great way to stay attracted to each other.

Love Tip:

It is important to try to get your schedule flexible so that natural urges for sex can occur. Spontaneous is definitely a turn on rather than making appointments to spend quality time with your partner.

Communicate

Intimacy begins long before the two of you go to bed and consists in sharing details regarding your day. This will help keep the lines open in the bedroom as well. If things are not going well in other areas of the relationship, then it will show up in the bedroom. For example, chores and other household responsibilities, including financial commitments can be a bit of a challenge. Therefore, it is important to communicate so that you can enjoy intimacy.

Spend Time Together

Before going to bed each night, spend quality time together with your partner. That is a great way for you to show that you care and set the pace for the evening ahead.

Love Tip:

This would be a great time to spend with God and continue to set relationship goals. Spirituality in a relationship is the foundation.

The Benefits of Being in a Supportive Relationship

When in a supportive relationship, you feel connected and happy as well as fulfilled. Active connection with others is what makes life more fulfilling, bringing our way health and happiness. So, what are the ways in which you can be supportive in a relationship? Here are some of them:

Listen

One of the most efficient ways for one to show regard and care for another is through listening. It is a form of support that leaves the other person feeling valued. Active listening to your partner indicates that you care about the thing that your partner communicates with you.

Dedicate Your Time to One Another

Being there for another person by setting time apart together establishes the ground for a stronger connection between you two. When you make time to be together with an individual you make room for building a healthy relationship in the time and energy devoted therein.

Communicate Effectively

It is not fair to assume the other person understands what you mean to say through your words. Ensure understanding is in place when you talk to them by use of proper communication skills. It is particularly important in a relationship requiring the support of both partners for each other.

Embrace Your Differences

People have a diverse way of perceiving things, and it is what makes us different as individuals. Appreciate that your partner sees things in a different angle thus does not want to do things your way. When you recognize the differences existing between you two, you communicate support in a very real manner. Remember that you will most likely get drawn to a person who is your opposite.

Communicate Trust

Trust is vital in a relationship and should get cultivated. Show trust to your partner by communicating the same through your interaction with him. Trust gets expressed through the way that you relate to each other, and you need to be sure it is what you send forth to your partner each time.

When utilized properly you will be able to show support to your partner through the various ways. Make use of them without holding back, thus entirely improving your relationship.

Why Taking Responsibility for Your Part of the Relationship is Key

The direction of a relationship gets determined by the way each person involved takes responsibility for his or her role in it. When each of you fully understands his or her part and is accountable to the other, you can embrace change and the resulting growth in the relationship. A positive approach that is more efficient to help reach relationship goals helps you take on responsibility without blaming each other.

Avoid Blame

When things go wrong, the easy option is to push blame on the other. It might be the other person had something to do with the outcome, but it should not be an excuse for you to avoid taking action. Assume the responsibility to ensure a better outcome next time around by exploring all aspects of the situation at hand.

Love Tip:

Calm Down and write in your emotional intimacy. It will save you from saying the wrong things to further complicate things in your relationship.

Focus on What You Can Change

When something happens in your relationship, there is often something you can do to create a change. Knowing the difference between what you can and cannot change, then concentrating on what you can, is part of the responsibility involved in relationships. Quit concentrating on what you have no power to change and instead focus on what you can.

Accept Your Part

You have a part to play in the relationship, and you'll do well to know what it is you can affect in it. Having understood this, you need to go on and take action to bring the change to it. The willingness to go ahead and do something is what matters when it comes to your responsibility in the relationship.

Focus On a Solution

When issues come up in a relationship, you should look towards finding a solution rather than concentrating on the problem. Where your focus is, it will determine how well you can get over issues in the relationship. You need to take responsibility for finding a solution, then go ahead and do it.

Life is Not Fair

If you focus on the fairness of life, you could lose the mark in your relationship. Rather, recognize that you have a role to play in the way your life turns out and ultimately affect the direction your relationship takes.

At the end of the day, you have to do what is best for you. This may be difficult at first, but you have to love yourself enough to do the right thing. When you love someone, you set him or her free. If he or she comes back, then you know it's real and what you need to do to honor yourself. If he or she comes back, then you know it's real and what you need to do to honor yourself. That's how you do what is best for the love of you.

Chapter 5:
MAKING PROGRESS IN A RELATIONSHIP

Over time, every relationship will change and evolve, shaping itself around your affinities, and shaping you in turn. For understanding this process, it is important for you to know the five stages of relationships.

The Stages of a Relationship

Just as there are stages in most human experiences, so they exist in relationships. The period between one such stage and the next depends on the emotional maturity of the two and also how compatible they are with one another. Here then are the five steps;

Stage #1: This is the One!

You think that you have found your ideal partner.

It is the start of a relationship during which partners get to know each other and the attraction between the two cannot be denied. Everything about the other person appears

---

perfect, and the stage could stretch from months to years. Since the two spend a lot of time together, a conflict has no place yet for them. It is all about fun, but this stage has to eventually make way for the next.

Stage #2: Who in the World is This?
Sooner or later reality will start to sneak into the relationship.

You begin to see 'crazy' and wonder why you are even dealing with this person. There must be something wrong with you too. The truth is we all got issues. You just got to figure out which ones you want to deal with in a relationship. The one who appeared faultless to you before is tainted with flaws about which you did not previously know. Even though still in love, it is not the same as before. Endorphins that are responsible for the sensation of being in love have started leveling off from a high.

Love Tip:
Keep working on yourself so that you can give your partner, your best self!

Stage #3: I Don't Like When...You Did Both!
Disappointment sets in at this stage when arguments begin to happen.

You can expect to have periods of no talking and stepping away may be the best situation. It doesn't matter how small a thing is but might cause anger due to differences between them, making it seem as if these is no hope. The thought of breaking up might occur at this time, and it takes effective communication and teamwork for things to work for the relationship.

Stage #4: Ok, I think I Understand You, But We Cool For Now!

Through their time together after the disappointment stage, the couple enters into stability.

Having found ways to work on any differences and with memories made together, it is now time to rest. The love shared between them allows for a connection that allows them to work through anything. Simply put, the phase where your heart was all over the place regarding your partner is over, but there remains a strong connection between you two.

Stage #5: Ok, We On The Same Page Now...

Commitment is the stage whereby couples accept each other flaws and all.

Each is content with the other, and together they make a great team. The future includes the other person in it, and plans can be done to be together. Both have matured and now enjoy their love together.

Next, let's take a look at how you should approach some very important matters when it comes to progressing your relationship towards that level of stability: The material plane.

The Strategies for Discussing Finances When Dating

One of the most important conversations you should have with the person you are dating as soon as things begin taking a more serious turn is finances. You need to know the financial status of the one you are dating well before committing. Discussing this altogether important topic requires tact as well as planning. A few tips to that end go a long way.

Reality Check:

Everybody lies or let's just say stretches the truth during Stage #1. Listen closely so you can hear the truth.

Set a date to discuss your finances.

This is a sure way for you both to share your plans regarding money. You might also need to do a bit of digging to find out how your partner is doing in this regard. No reason being slapped with surprises later on when you realize your partner has a loan he is servicing without you knowing about it.

Offer to share information in hope for an exchange.

You can put down your financial commitments and then share them with your partner, with the goal to have them share similar information regarding finances with you. Or, try a more gentle approach if your partner is shy about discussing the matter. In this case, you will need to talk him or her into it after you share your details.

Get them to talk about finances through a few questions.

Perhaps you can start off asking for an opinion regarding some of the money-saving tips. Or even inquire of your partner's view in connection with making an investment and credit position. The aim is to get him to reveal his position regarding matters to do with credit and finances in general.

You want to ask questions that will let you see their ability to think about money both short and long term.

On the next page, you will find a few questions to help you get started.

Conversation Starter Questions about Finances
1. What strategies do you use to save for something small, such as a new washer or something that cost at least $500 or more?
2. Where do you see yourself financially in the next five years?
3. How much do you save each month? What does that look like?
4. How do you feel about investments?
5. Do you like credit cards? Why or why not?
6. How would you use your credit to help you build wealth?
7. If you see something you want, then do you get it right away or save for it? Why or why not?

These questions will get the conversation started about finances and then sit back and observe what you can to see if their responses match their actions.

Exchange financial past with your date.

Take a walk down memory lane by volunteering ways in which you have been able to get through financially. The bottom line is to get a hint of the spending habits of the person. For instance, discuss how you managed to go through college with an aim to gaining knowledge of their values regarding finances. Another example is to discuss how you had to budget for whatever reason to demonstrate your ability to manage money.

Discuss financial styles.

For example, ask your partner if he or she waits to pay their bills at the last minute or if they do so well in advance. A well-balanced checkbook is a good lead to the kind of person your partner is.

The Reasons Why Prenuptial Conversations in Dating Matter

Before two people tie the knot, it is important for them to have a good and long talk beforehand. This talk is meant for partners to learn about marriage expectations of each other before committing to be together. No matter the stage of the relationship, it is vital to hold this conversation with your partner. Here are some reasons why:

Equality

Between the two of you, each should be aware of the way the other defines justice. It helps to put in place what is expected from each of you so as to see the success of the relationship.

Divorce or Death

The death of a partner can bring on a lot of confusion, especially if there is no preset agreement regarding what happens in the event. Same goes for divorce, as it can also throw the lives of the two involved in disarray. Discuss such eventualities with your partner to avoid stress should this happen in the future.

Property and Liabilities

Any assets owned by either of the two should have an agreement made over what happens once they get married. The same works for debts and other liabilities, so that one partner is not forced to take up the burden of the other, carried into the marriage.

Career Path

After the wedding, a spouse might have to change his or her career path to pursue alternative openings. For instance, one might decide to quit work in order to take care of the affairs of the family. Having an agreement on this issue in place prevents conflict that might occur when this happens.

Retirement

Two people planning on getting married need to discuss life after retirement. Issues such as pension plan, property, and owning a home need to be taken up so as to avoid being caught up in time. Planning ahead is advised and should be considered as an important part of planning together.

Talk about these issues as the relationship goes along. Bring them up when you are just about to tie the knot does not help. It should be done in a setting that is comfortable for the two of you.

Love Tip:

You want to discuss outside of the bedroom or even the house. You may want to suggest coffee talks or lunch dates to discuss these matters. If your partner is not willing to do this, this is a huge warning sign because this person is not mature enough to take these issues seriously. You may want to wait before you commit to him or her.

Signs to Observe when Dating a Divorced Person

Just because a person is divorced, it is not justifiable to disregard getting involved with them. A little knowledge about the individual will help you make a decision regarding the possibility of such a relationship. Among others, be sure to observe these signs:

The Relationship between Him or Her and the Ex

Ties that come in being married to another do not fade away once the divorce gets finalized. There are memories that do not go away after signing the divorce. The Ex remains a part of the life of your new partner, and you should be ready for that. Still, try to find out if your partner is done with them so you can have a basis to build a relationship.

Love Tip:

The partner must set the boundaries. If you see that he or she cannot, then you may want to re-evaluate whether you would want to enter such a relationship.

Readiness to Commit

Divorce comes with loads of emotional baggage and you do not want to get caught up with it. It helps if you date a person who is well ahead in the process, as there will be less of the past being carried into the relationship. Divorce is terrible, and you do not want to be the one to nurse the other through the process. Unless, of course, you are up for it!

No Need to Rush

Your date is probably going through a lot accepting the divorce. It is safe for you not to expect too much too soon from a person who might still be hurting from the impact of such a devastating process. Take time before seeking information on the same.

Time on His Own

After the divorce, your date will probably keep in contact with the ex for various reasons. In a case where kids are involved, you will have to contend with spending time alone at times while he goes to be with the kids. You may not spend as much time as you'd like to together, after all.

Honesty

You might notice times when your date tends to keep to himself. In those times, it is right to find out what is going on in his mind by encouraging him to discuss it with you. Well, not every detail, as you risk getting overwhelmed.

Family and Friends

They may not like you much to start with, viewing you as one come to take the place of the former spouse. Keep an open mind and do not judge them, after all, they know the Ex better than they do you.

The Reasons Why You Should Keep People Out of Your Business

For someone who has other people entangled with their personal affairs, it becomes difficult to have personal space. It is essential to set a limit on the level of your personal life that people have access to at any time. Otherwise, you might end up having too much information in the wrong hands and being unable to do anything about it. Let's have a look at some of the reasons for you to keep people out of your business:

Not Everyone Shares Your Joy

You know the feeling of accomplishment at having achieved that goal. You are tempted to let the world know how happy that makes you feel but wait a minute. How many people are going to celebrate your success with you? Chances are, there might be someone who will not share your joy, but get the opportunity to ruin it instead. This proves that the less you share, the less the risk of it leaking out.

Opinions that are Uncalled For

The minute you let others in on your affairs, you open yourself up to hear what they have to say. Your business is just that, yours, and it is best left that way if you do not want to get unpleasant opinions from other people.

Shield the Wrongs

When things go wrong with your business, as sometimes they will, it is easier for you to deal with if fewer people know the details of them. In an example where a relationship you are involved in hits the rocks, it will be easier to deal with the blow without having to explain it to the world.

Pressure to Maintain

When people know what goes on with your business, you get under pressure to deliver. It is especially troublesome when a relationship is involved. What happens between you and your partner should not be the business of others, but the two of you. To keep it that way you have to safeguard the information you offer.

No Taking Back

In the era of social media, what you share on the World Wide Web is not easy to get back. Think about it: You may not be able to delete what you share with the world. Be determined to keep your business to yourself to avoid any regrets this might cause you later on.

Chapter 6:
THE COMMON CATEGORIES OF PEOPLE IN A RELATIONSHIP

As human beings, we have a tendency to put labels onto other people, categorizing them into little boxes that we can give meaning to and assign a role in our life. Consciously or not, we all use these categories in different relationships, so let us take a look at which common categories your partner could assign to you, and which you can use to realize how you feel about certain people.

What Does It Mean to Be Called a Queen or a King?

Giving the names of Queen or King does not just happen in a relationship as they have some qualities attached to them. To be a queen or king you have to fulfill certain conditions. They are what qualify you to be known by the name by your partner. Some of them include self-mastery and maturity which are vital for any relationship.

Mature people are dependable in a love relationship and keep their word. When something needs to be said, they say it without holding back, with love. It is everything in a love relationship and involves making wise decisions for the benefit of the relationship. You are patient to watch your love grow through working at it together so it can blossom with time. It takes the knowledge that nothing happens at once and that people grow into a relationship with time and with the help of one another.

A mature person will go a long way to making an accomplishment in the relationship. You are not afraid to put in work to make the relationship grow and are committed to making things work out well between the two of you. On the other hand, an immature individual is under constant change in life.

Self-mastery, on the other hand, is taking control of the thought processes that chart the way you behave. You do not react to situations but rather employ reason in the way in which you respond. There are several steps involved in self-mastery and include among others, making peace with your past for a more objective view of the present and future. It also means keeping tabs with the way that you behave so as to allow growth and change.

Once you cultivate these vices in life, you automatically deserve the title Queen or King. Much of it involves an in-depth look into the recesses of life to determine a more positive outlook on life. It shows in the way you package yourself to love and ultimately affects the outcome of the relationship. All focus is on having the right qualities to steer the relationship to success.

Why Women Put Men into These Categories: King, Big Daddy or Handsome

In each man she dates, a woman attaches a particular value to a man. Different men are viewed differently by a woman mainly due to the way they come across to her. Throughout her life, a woman might have the chance to encounter different men in her life, all viewed from different angles in her eyes. To understand better what she sees in you, here's a run-down of the different titles women use.

King

The girl has seen something worth some respect in you. You are at a higher place of value with her and have won her respect. In the eyes of a woman, a King does all meant to do and more. If you are taking care of her and still manage to keep her interested, you deserve to be King in her life.

Big Daddy

Some women like to call their men Big Daddy when having sex. It has nothing to do with a father; rather it means that he is the boss and she views him as a protector and as one who is in charge. What it means is that the man is in charge and has hit the right buttons with her. If she screams out `Big Daddy" during those intimate moments you've got something to pride yourself in, brother!

Handsome

You are most probably older than she is with a face that is attractive but also mature. Women take maturity to mean experience thus views the man as one who knows what he is doing. This is somewhat attractive to women, as no one wants a man who still fumbles around in the presence of a woman. A handsome man is sophisticated and combines it well with his looks.

The name a woman gives a man tells a lot about the way the two relate to each other. One can always know his place in a woman's heart by the way she addresses him. You might want to listen for the name she calls you next time you manage to curl her toes!

Why Men Put Women into Categories such as Main Chick and Side Chick

Men like to categorize the women in their lives depending on the function in their lives. For mention, let's take a look at the **main girl**.

She is well known to the man and has been around for a while. He finds comfort with her and sees the possibility of taking things further with her. The two are together most of the time and might even consider living together. He has taken her to meet his family and does not mind having a baby with her. In his mind, she is the one who best suits being his wife and the mother of his kids.

With the time of the two being together, however, the actual colors of the woman begin to show. No longer is she only interested in satisfying her man having got comfortable in her position. He starts to see a change in her as she does not have to hide her real self any longer. The man sees an entirely different person from whom he knew, and the stress of his commitment to her makes him long for an escape. Enter the **side chick**.

She offers him everything the main girl does, cleaning, cooking, and sex. Communication with her is top-notch, and he couldn't ask for better anywhere else. Her life is often one big lie as she may not know of the main chick. All she's aware of is that she gets treated well and she reciprocates his feelings too. There is one who knows of the main chick yet does not mind at all. She is the type that is not after anything serious with the man and prefers to keep things casual.

Unlike women, men can cheat on a woman they love without any emotions involved. It might be that all a man needs from the other woman is only sexual satisfaction. Or it could be he gets attracted to another physically.

Depending on the way a woman meets the need of a man she thus gets regarded accordingly. It has to do with the diverse requirements of a man in a lady and how one goes about fulfilling them.

10 Signs That You Are a Side Chick or a Boo Thang

Here is a list of some things that will signal that you are his side chick:

He doesn't seem anxious to show you off to his friends and keeps you out of the limelight.

Most likely he does not want to get caught with you by the main chick. On a walk down the street, he does not even hold your hand. He is probably scared someone who knows his real chick might see him.

At a certain time each week he does not want anything to do with you.

It is most likely because he is with the other woman. If he'd rather see you on weeknights, it is probably because his weekends get reserved for someone else.

You have not met any member of his family.

He doesn't think you are the kind of girl his folks should know.

He avoids calling you by name and would rather use endearments so that he does not mix up your name.

Worse still, is if he has saved you with a fake name on his phone.

You don't get invited to spend the night at his place.

Do not take it for granted he does not want to cuddle up for the evening. That may not be your position in his life.

Late night texts only?

You might be seeing a man whose only interest in you is getting laid. A sure sign you do not qualify as his main chick.

He prefers texting to talking to you on the phone.

Most likely he does not want to be heard by his woman talking to you. Texting is easier.

You never get to touch his phone.

Most likely he has photos of his girl and does not want you to see them.

He prefers coming over.

A good sign he is hiding you from someone is when he prefers coming over to your place. You never get invited to his place nor does he take you out in public often enough.

You don't get to see him during major holidays.

Come Christmas time, and especially Valentine's Day, your man is missing. Not once but often enough to have you thinking he has someone more important to host them.

Chapter 7:
WHAT WE REALLY WANT IN A RELATIONSHIP

L et's face it: Men and women look for different things in a relationship. Something you want may not be a priority for your partner, and the other way around. It is important to communicate with your partner about your priorities, likes and dislikes, but it's also valuable to know what men and women want in general.

Let us take a look at some of those things.

Men Want Respect; Women Want Love

Respect is to a man what love is to a woman. When you respect the man in your life, you validate him in the sense that he feels valued to you and other people. The absence of this makes it better for him to be alone and without love than being forced to suffer disrespect. It might appear not so important to a woman because all she needs is love. Some reasons why respect is everything to a man and love to a woman;

Respect for your husband is affirmation, which is something he needs.

At the end of the day, after being out in the world, he will need to feel accepted through the encouragement that you give. When he feels accepted, he will more likely be open to you.

Respect communicates your belief in him.

Even when he has made a mistake, your partner needs to know that he is still a hero in your eyes. Your consideration goes a long way in making him better able to be the man you want him to be.

Respect allows openness in a man.

You need to show him respect so that he can feel safe to let you into his thoughts. You may be astonished to learn how many negative thoughts go through his mind each day and showing respect helps him feel in charge. It is a primal need for a man to feel this way in a relationship.

Love speaks affirmation to a woman in a relationship.

Unlike a man, the woman takes your words rather seriously. A husband who uses words generously communicate love to his wife will have done a huge part in the relationship.

Love makes a woman explore her potential.

You've heard it said that when you love a woman, there is no limit to what she can achieve. It is the driving force as it serves to endorse her worth to get things done. Simply loving your wife will give her wings to fly and you can enjoy the fruits it brings.

Dating Like a Man: How to Play Hardball

There are times during the dating game when a woman has to come down hard about what she wants from the man she likes. It entails taking on some of the habits men have when dating.

Even though it is not the natural way of doing things since women like to get pursued, it may be the only way to have the man in your life commit to the relationship.

So you've decided to go at it with no holds barred. Your mind gets set on the goal, and that is to win him over at whatever cost. It might involve a bit of rough play for you, but you do not give much thought to it.

As long as you end up together with the man, you are set on using whatever method there is to lay hold of him and keep him.

For a man, dating is about the chase to get the woman of one's choice. More often than not, some few dirty tricks can be used to make sure the two are together. Quite contrary to a lady who uses emotions to get through to the man. When she has to adopt the style usually employed by a man, a woman is taking on something that is outside her territory in the dating game. She has decided to take on the pursuit of a man instead of sitting around waiting for it to happen to her. Most people view aggression as the role of a man, but it is one the woman who has decided to play hardball has to utilize to ensure she gets what she wants at the end of the day.

Most of the methods used in the process far surpass what usually accepted of such a woman. For instance, asking a man out instead of waiting for him to do it can be viewed as part of the package. As is, detailing her expectations to him before the two get involved with each other. Nothing is out of her way when a woman decides to play hardball and go win over a man she likes. After all, she has to know that she is the prize. Her feminine energy must lead the way, along with her actions. Actions speak louder than words.

Chapter 8:
DEALING WITH CONFLICTS IN A RELATIONSHIP

Conflict can be both good and bad for a relationship. Resolving the problems that arise between you and your partner can help strengthen the relationship. On the other hand, sometimes the conflicts can't be bridged. In these cases, it's important to know when to compromise, and when to start thinking about moving on.

In this chapter, we are going to take a look at some of the major issues that may arise when a relationship hits the wall.

Men Are Intimidated by Strong Women

There are quite a few reasons why men are frightened by strong women. They are what make it close to impossible for the relationship to go as it should. They have to deal with the woman being in touch with her feelings and not settling for less. It could rub off the wrong way to a man who thinks he has to influence a woman. So what are these reasons men get intimidated by strong women?

Such a woman is not one to remain silent on matters concerning her. You will know when you rub her the wrong way as she will not take to let you make her feel inferior. She will do what is pleasing to her and is not willing to change for you. It stems from a strong belief in herself as she knows what is right for her.

Another characteristic of this kind of woman is that she easily moves on in life. When she discovers that there is no point holding on to something that is not working, then she prefers to let go of it. Men view her as impatient, but she is only well aware of what works for her. It's all or nothing with her, and if you can't give her the whole deal in the relationship, she moves on. Not one to get coerced into silence, she remains active in the values she holds strong.

You probably know a woman who does nothing to hide how she feels. The kind that does not shy off saying how they feel so that she does not appear crazy. That's a strong woman right there, and you might be surprised at how deep her feeliings run. She is also in touch with her intuition, knowing what is right for her at all times. Her feelings matter, therefore, she will only stay if you fit in with them.

Everything about the woman speaks emotion and more of it. She is passionate of all she does and will not withhold her thoughts of it. It is what scares most men as they are less emotional beings. Therefore, Men who are desiring strong women must learn how to express themselves emotionally.

Five Signs That Your Partner Does Not Support Your Life's Work

Partners are the best to support each other in all aspects of life. When it does not happen, it can be the cause of some issues in the relationship. One of the areas you need to support your partner is regarding his or her life's work.

A person's vocation is important to them as it is what takes care of his or her needs. It should, therefore, matter to both of them as it will affect their lifestyle. It becomes difficult to prosper in your work if you have a partner who does not support you. Here are some signs that tell that your partner does not support your life work.

He does not get into a discussion regarding your job.

You come home stressed about work issues and expect him to hear you out. On the contrary, he does not want to discuss anything related to your job.

Neither does he acknowledge any development in that area.

Forget about rushing home with news of your promotion or that business deal you clinched as you will most likely face a stony silence. If lucky, a few grunts are all you get.

He is not proud of your accomplishments.

We all know that a partner that is proud of what the other does will not stop talking about it to friends, right? If you find his friends always asking what you do, then be sure he is not letting them know. And it is not because he does not know, but he simply thinks it is not the right thing for you to do.

He keeps suggesting options.

Your partner does not stop pointing out openings for you to consider despite the fact that you are doing something already. What he is communicating to you is that you do not have his support with it.

He tries to discourage you.

Has your partner warned you of what might happen at your current work? Perhaps a way for him to discourage you, with a hope that you pick up the cue and leave the work. It might work for the partner who takes the others' word as a rule.

Dealing with Discovering the New Layers of the Person That Is Your Partner: Your Strategy

Relationships evolve with time, and notable changes occur in the two involved. Part of what happens is inevitable as people change with time. The direction of it depends on the willingness of both partners to adjust to each other as they happen. It is the mark of understanding that only the two that are knowledgeable on the fact will embrace. There are a few strategies for use to ensure you are prepared to take on changes in your partner. Here are some of them:

Embrace it.

It is bound to happen with time, and the sooner you accept it, the better. Due to the versatility of life, you can expect your partner to change, just as you too will. Of importance, it is for you to keep an open mind all through when it happens. One way for you to do this is a willingness to adjust.

Accept it.

Nothing stays the same and as seasons change so do people. Your partner will change with time and to avoid conflict you need to accept that it will happen. Offering support to your partner in the process will do good for you two.

Look out for red lights.

The cause of change in your partner could signal he might be going through trouble. Therefore, you should pay attention to any changes. Ensure you create an open forum to express any concerns you might have.

Chase after it.

Not all change is bad, and you might need to spice up life with a few of it. Try out different stuff with your partner and watch the way your relationship revives. At times, it is what is needed to keep the glow.

A new look at conflict

It will happen once in a while since you are both changing. It is of the essence to ensure it does not bring division between you two. Step away from repeated patterns and look for new ways to deal with it.

Indeed change does occur in any relationship, and it takes effort of the two to understand how best to deal with it. The relationship depends on it.

Dealing with a Partner Who Uses the Silent Treatment: What to Do?

When disagreements occur between two people, each has his or her way of dealing with it. Proper communication often gives them common ground so that there is the agreed method of resolution. It could, however, be absent. This can present a challenge because miscommunication can lead to more separation, silence, and a future argument as each partner may decide to use words against each other.

The silent treatment is common among couples everywhere, yet it has one of the most destructive effects on relationships. It is when a partner decides to shut the other off. There is no communication between you two, and it is as if you do not exist in the mind of your partner.

You need to realize that a partner will use this to try and gain control. You have nothing to do with his uncertainty and should not burden yourself with guilt.

One good way to deal with it is to get on with life as if you do not notice. You do not want to make it appear as if the silent treatment is working, therefore, ignore it, and get on as if you do not notice. Most likely, he will come around when he sees it does not bother you.

A common mistake partners of such people make is to try to figure the thoughts of the other. At some point, he will need to share his thoughts so why bother trying to figure them out anyway?

Your partner will most likely go silent on you after you make a demand he feels unable to meet. It might be emotional or else, but the thing is he seems incapable of achieving it thus results in going silent on you.

You might want to check how he feels about the request. Hopefully, he will shed some light on the matter and choose to be less demanding.

It can be quite a hassle to live with a person who results to the silent treatment as a way to address issues. It is pretty much like he wishes away the issue at hand and does not see the need to do anything else about it. He is probably thinking about himself more thus results to doing things the way that best suits him.

Dealing with Forgiveness in a Relationship: How to Move Forward

It is said forgiveness is the oil of relationships as it keeps the wheels moving throughout. No doubt you need to make use of it to ensure you remain together. It all depends on the issue at hand as at times you might be unable to forgive each other. It is advised that you do since both of you will need to bear with each other over time, especially if you have children together.

One thing for sure is you need to walk in forgiveness attitude most of the time. Remember not to use confrontation as it is likely to lead to more damage, but discuss the matter amicably between two of you. Might be difficult at times, given what your partner has done for you, but it is worth the while.

When you are the recipient of forgiveness from your spouse, you would like to have the issue behind you then move forward together. The same expected of you should you be the one who gets wronged. Remember all along that you have a relationship to uphold and your feelings should not reign over everything. Some things are too trivial to hold onto once you've forgiven your partner. In the larger ones, it is good to remember that what is most important is the love you have for each other.

An attitude that works anytime is one where you have predetermined to forgive your partner way ahead of time. It doesn't matter what he does to you after that; you do not hold on to it but rather have your mind set on forgiveness. It will spare you a lot of extreme concern and also give freedom to your partner when you are more forgiving of his faults.

As opposed to holding grudges, forgiving your partner has redeeming qualities as you do not have to hold on to negative emotion but rather let go and move on. It is good for your wellbeing in the end, as you do not have to carry destructive emotions with you all the time. Choose to let go of any hurt and work at making your relationship better with time.

Wisdom from Minister Alise

It never ceases to amaze me at how we as humans have a hard time forgiving others. Forgiveness is the hardest life lesson that we all have to encounter. When you think about forgiveness, it is important for you to understand that forgiveness is for you. Each of us have sinned so you can't condemn others for their trespassing because you too have trespassed against others. The bible says it best, "For if you forgive others their trespasses, your heavenly Father will also forgive you" (Matthew 6:14). I must let you know that it may take some time, but let your heart be free to love again by making a choice to honor forgiveness.

Chapter 9:
THE MIND GAMES MEN PLAY IN A RELATIONSHIP

Sometimes, it turns out that the person you entered into a relationship with is not who you thought he was. Not all men are manipulative, but it's extremely important for you to know how to recognize when a man plays games in a relationship.

The Mind Games Men Play

A man that is not willing to commit can have many ways to deal with the woman with whom he is involved. Mind games are used to send mixed signals as a way to play around with someone's emotions. There are many reasons men do that, and these include for the mere fun of seeing the woman get disoriented.

Then there are some who like to test the waters regarding the emotions of a woman. Others play mind games when they have something they want from a woman. Whatever the reason there are many mind games that men play.

Demands

Do you suddenly find that your man starts to make demands that are way out of the ordinary? Is he enforcing new rules in the relationship? He might be playing with your mind for the mere reason of knowing how understanding you are. Your adaptability is on the test, and you better give him a good reason to win his trust.

Ceases to communicate with you

It happens when a man neither calls nor picks your calls. He makes no effort to keep in touch leaving you with a multitude of questions in mind. Try to stay calm while all the while communicating caring towards him. He may not respond, but you have made a mark on him by reaching out to show your commitment to him.

Silent treatment and limited communication

A man might go silent on you, showing no sign of wanting to talk to you. Either that or only talks to you when necessary. A yes or no might be all that you get when you initiate conversation with him. Relax and let endurance show.

Aggression

Are you concerned your man has suddenly become aggressive? Fear not, all he might be doing is testing your resilience in the relationship.

Comparison

No woman wants the man they love to compare them with someone else. It doesn't matter if it is a relative in question, yet a man can do it to make clear his expectations of you. You might want to try and check what he sees in the person in question.

How to Recognize when a Man Wants to Use You

It may not be easy to know the intentions the man you are seeing has towards you, but with time, the signs will be evident to you. A man who is only interested in using you is after what's in it for him.

You are likely to recognize him from the questions he poses to you after you meet him. Most likely he will want to know about your income, job, and even the type of car that you drive. All aimed at knowing how he can fit in to take advantage of you. Here are sure signs to help recognize such a man.

He makes it hard for you to say no to him.

A man who is after using you will use power play to make demands on you. You find it difficult saying no to him as he makes it seem like doom to you. A man who makes you act out of fear is most certainly using you.

Good only when in need.

Is your man all friendly and kind only when he wants something from you? He will offer to help you out and go out of his way for some time, but as soon as you grant his request, he is nowhere to be seen. Be warned; you are in the company of a user.

Guilt tripping.

So he has run a small errand for you and now's your time to recompense. What he wants is bigger in comparison, but he does not hesitate to remind you of the favor he did you so that you feel obliged to help him out. What a user!

He leaves you feeling resentment towards him

It is because you are not in a balanced relationship and all he wants is to have his needs met. It's as if your needs does not matter. The man is only after having his met and does not even want to hear about yours. Should you bring it up, you either get ignored or get shelved as having an irrelevant need. It is all about him, remember?

Scenario: "Oh, It's Like That? I Got You Now!"

John is dating Jennifer and it is going on seven months. John started out being prince charming and catering to Jennifer whenever she needed him. About five months into the relationship, John started ignoring Jennifer by not responding to her text-messages and reducing his visits to her. They were not arguing, but John shared with her a post that Jennifer had put on her social media. The post read:

"Don't take kindness for granted. When you love someone, You don't wish him or her well. You follow your heart for your own happiness and let the chips fall where they may. Love is the most powerful force on Earth. I didn't lose you...You lost me...You'll search for me in everyone you're with...I won't be found."

After John read that post, he sent a text message to Jennifer wishing her well. At first, Jennifer was hurt because she really want to see their connection grow. After much thought, Jennifer decided that she would do exactly what John had told her. She was tired of his mind games and temper tantrums, as if he was three years old. So, Jennifer did the unthinkable—she moved on as he suggested and left John for someone else to deal with.

Love Tip:

Re-evaluate this. As a woman, you were born to create. Therefore, this type of energy only suppresses and will only impact your second chakra. It is important to be heard, even if action is not taken.

Chapter 10: APPROACHING THE END OF THE RELATIONSHIP

There may come a time when, even with your best efforts to keep the spark alive, the relationship falls into a rut from which it's impossible to dig it out. It is important for you to understand the factors that lead to this kind of a situation, as well as what to do when the relationship inevitably has to reach its end.

The Mistakes That Lead to the Loss of Interest in the Partner

A number of errors present when two people are dating, and they often spell consequences on the relationship. They can, however, be avoided if a person knows himself setting boundaries where a relationship is concerned. Five of the most glaring mistakes people that are dating make include:

Going too far too fast

So you've met this person whom you have a connection with and feel tempted to let him into the dark recesses of your heart. Beware of telling too much too fast as it might work against your relationship. It takes the time to form a healthy relationship and involves time and patience. Anything that is worthwhile will take a chance to build, and this is right about relationships as well.

Making it all about feelings

A relationship that gets built on these will hardly go anywhere as these cannot be trusted. Feelings come and go, and you should have much more to base it on for a more solid background.

The reign of fear

A relationship that comes into being due to the fear of being alone is certainly one that will not go far. There are many reasons people get involved with others and fear could be one of them. When you are scared of what will happen if you do not get involved with another means you are making a huge mistake.

Sex

When you sleep with another person, you form a bond that might be difficult to break. It is not right to use sex as a way to get involved with another as you might get disappointed when the other person does not share your feelings. Sex can cheat you into seeing what is not in another person such as the desire to get committed to you.

While you have your own free will, it is important to really think about whether you are ready to deal with the challenges that intimacy brings. For example, you need to assess or have a plan in place on how you would proceed if the person does not share your same feelings. There's nothing sexy about being rejected. After all, you are a prize.

Ambiguous bonds

You see each other, but it's not clear where you are headed. You can go as far as sleeping together, but there is no sign that either or one of you wants to commit. Quite a sorry state as you will most likely end up on the losing end after wasting time together.

Scenario: "Yeah, I see a Future With Us"

Christopher and Summer dated for three years. Chris was everything that a woman could ask for, but over time things changed. Summer was getting out of a relationship and wanted friendship; Chris provided that to her. Two years into the relationship, Summer realized that Chris was still married and had been married for almost 20 years. Summer was hurt and she regretted that she had been intimate with him for all these years. Chris took Summer to meet his children and Summer got a chance to see that Rodenda and Him were truly separated and had been for well over 10 years, but Summer wondered why did he keep it a secret. Summer began to see the light, but she was not ready to leave him quite yet. They had booked a trip together and they needed that time to get away. That was their first trip together and she just knew in her heart that he was planning a future for them. Three months later, Chris and Summer were in the Caribbean and that's when Summer learned the truth about him and his situation. He was still married to Rodenda because he was an illegal immigrant and needed to get citizenship. Summer also learned about two other women named Cheryl and Jody. Those women were not who Chris said they were. Summer only found out about them because they called his cellphone and he took both calls. It was in that moment that Chris' eyes told it all. Summer ended things once they made it back to the United State of America.

Words of Wisdom from Minister Dr. Alise

Even if you feel that you have wasted time in a relationship, it is important to know that nothing is truly wasted. Both Summer and Chris attracted each other to work on some life lessons and experience life blessings. Summer is just mad right now, but I would recommend that she talks to a life coach (Hey Summer, I'm Available to help you process that relationship. Email or Text our office).

Why You Should Move Forward Without Closure if the Person Doesn't Share

At times relationships do come to an end, and when they do each person goes his way. It is a nagging need for one to know the cause of the breakup so as to get closure. It entails both partners holding a conversation so as to communicate what went wrong in the relationship. At times it may not be possible if either of the two does not see the need to put things to rest through communication. In which case it calls for the other to move on without knowing what went wrong.

A closure is when you come to the acknowledgment that things are over between you two.

There are some reasons for you to move forward even without closure.

Come to terms with the fact it is over between you two.

There is no reason for you hanging on to the hope of getting back with the person. Be kind to yourself and let them go to allow yourself move on into something new.

Closure helps the healing process after the breakup.

No doubt it is painful losing someone who meant a lot to you. It may be impossible for you to detach from them so quickly especially without knowing the reason for the breakup. You, however, owe it to yourself to forgive yourself and seek to move on.

It is the ticket to getting your happiness back.

When you get the closure, you choose to rid yourself of bitterness thus open up chances to be happy again. You realize that instead of spending energy exchanging bitter words with your ex you can instead go in pursuit of fresh beginnings.

Your happiness depends on it.

Have you ever seen people who hang on to a relationship long after its dead? These are the ones who have placed their happiness in the hands of the one they were seeing and are unable to move on. Life does not stop after a relationship ends thus should seek happiness elsewhere.

You should move forward even though you've had no closure with your ex so as to be able to cut off the remaining attachments. Nothing works better to help forget what you previously had than to get busy with other things.

How to Walk Away from a Dead or Toxic Relationship

When in a relationship you might find that instead of being happy you are more of miserable. No matter what hold the relationship has on you, it could be the time that you made away so as to get back happiness in your life. You first need to recognize that you are unhappy being with someone before charting the way to get away from them.

No doubt it is okay to get used to someone you have been with for some time. Disentangling yourself from one is made harder by the emotions you have invested in the relationship. The first thing for you to do is to recognize it for what it is and then finding something to occupy your mind instead. Work or hobbies are what most people use.

You want what's best for you; therefore, there is no need for you to bear with something that's not working for you, right? Despite getting different views from those around you, family and friends included, it might be a good thing for you to hear your heart out. If the relationship is not working to make you a better person, then you could be happier without it.

Once you reach the decision to end a toxic relationship, you then need to stick to it with the help of others. No doubt you will need them to walk you through the painful process it entails and could use some positive activities in the process. Anything to reinforce your esteem that has been wounded by the process will help get you back on your feet soon enough.

Recognize not all relationships are meant to last as people, and circumstances change with time. Instead of beating yourself up for having been in a bad relationship, purpose to grow from it and move on with life. Ultimately, your happiness starts with you and the way you go about finding it after that determines how it goes.

It is no easy thing for one to walk away from a toxic relationship, but it might be the one thing needed to find yourself again.

Chapter 11:
DEALING WITH A RELATIONSHIP'S END IN A HEALTHY WAY

Dealing with breakups is hard, especially after you've invested so much time and energy into a person. There may be some unresolved issues, which may even continue to present a problem for you in the days, months or even years after the relationship ends. In this chapter, we will give you some tips on how to resolve such issues and avoid the pain of a messy breakup.

The Questions That Need to Be Answered after a Breakup

After you break up with someone, there are some questions you would like to have them answer. Lucky thing should you get closure after it ends as you can then raise some of them to your ex. Breakups hurt because you lose the relationship but also the hopes that you had of being together. There are five questions to ask after you break up with someone. Let's take a look at them on the next page.

Why?

Simple as it sounds you want to know why it ended. It doesn't matter if it turns to be unpleasant to you as you will at least know the reason why it ended. So he dumped you, making it clear he wants nothing to do with you anymore but just why did he do it?

Did you love me?

You most probably want to know if he had feelings for you to begin with. Was it just a fleeting feeling or did he love you? Or was it just a way for him to get something out of you when he could?

Do you miss me?

So you had some great times together while the relationship thrived. Perhaps even did some things you find difficult to do with someone else. Does he miss those moments like you do? What's the feeling when he does miss those times? Does he have the memory of the special times the two of you spent together?

Think of marrying me?

Perhaps he had not made his intentions known to you, in the first place. You are curious to know if he envisioned you as a life partner or was only joy riding with you.

Did you ever cheat on me?

So you thought you had him in the right place and then he turns around and says it's over between you two. Many questions go through your mind one of which is if he ever cheated on you with another while you were together. It makes it easier for you to move on once you get answers to the questions as you are in a better place to start over again. This might be a past-life connection so refer back to Chapter 3 about the various types of relationships in which you will experience in your lifetime.

How to Deal With a Controlling Ex: Your Place or His

Even after two people decide to go separate ways one of them is likely to have some feelings left for the other. It becomes complicated if your Ex is controlling as you will have to find a way to draw boundaries. No doubt it is not a good experience to have someone who not only belongs in your past but does not realize it too.

You probably wish you had nothing to do with the Ex anymore. Unfortunately, it might be necessary to see each other every so often. Mainly this is due to issues regarding children you have had together. It's of importance to have a middle ground so that his presence does not get in your way in any case. Consideration for this involves the decision about who should go to the others' place. One of you will have to make a move and an agreement on the same is needed. There are quite some factors for you to consider in this regard, including convenience.

If you decide, he comes over to your place be prepared to give up your space. A controlling Ex will most likely not toe the line regarding how far to go. You can expect an opinion or two, about stuff with which you do not need him to be involved. To your Ex, it is all about being in control whether it is necessary or not.

Should it be his place then you save yourself some trouble of him meddling in your affairs. However, you will need to bear with the thought that your child is under a different authority, one that is most likely different from your own. For instance, your house rules no longer need to apply, considering your

Ex will want to assert his authority on the child. He will most likely try to make it appear as if his place is a haven in comparison to yours.

In the circumstances, you will have to decide what works better for you. Is it better if he comes over at your place including all the perks or rather settles for his place? It is a choice for you to make depending on circumstances.

The Reasons Why Being Single Is a Good Season in Life

Being single is a splendid time in life for one to discover oneself. During this period when not entangled in a relationship, you can happily enjoy yourself in the season. Here are some of what it comes with the following:

Sense of self

When single you are more aware of yourself, without getting merged with another and risk losing sight of yourself. When you know what works for you, it is more likely for you to find happiness around you. You appreciate life in its simplicity with the security of knowing who you are.

Steer away from loneliness

You do not depend on another to complete you. It is possible to feel unfulfilled with a partner when you expect all needs to connect with them as they may not measure up. Being single allows you to spend time with some other people such as family and friends making it almost impossible for you to feel lonely.

Make your rules

In a relationship, people have a tendency to think of the other person ahead of themselves. Single life allows you to put yourself first and get down to living it out. You go by your rules, and no one can hold you back in exploring the things that most interest you in life. Perhaps only your inhibitions will hold you back, and even then you have freedom to choose how far you can go with things. With no rules in place, you get to enjoy the fullness of life uninhibited.

L⊙ve ṬỴp:

If you are dating, then it is important to ask questions to see how your partner fit into your established world. Remember, you cannot change your life purpose for a person and you definitely cannot change him or her. It has to be two people walking the same spiritual paths who are willing, ready, and able to learn and continue to grow spiritually.

Love yourself

It is critical for one to be comfortable in his skin before reaching out to another. People who love themselves can attract love to them. Not always do you need a partner to set the rules to your happiness as you can do it on your own. Being the best you can be will remove any limits in life.

Recharge

In the midst of other people, you spend a lot of energy in the activities it involves. You are required to participate and be mindful of their emotions while interacting with them. Nothing drains the mind of a man or woman like maintaining a connection with other people. When single, you can steer away from the emotional strain that comes with interacting with other people.

CONCLUSION

In this book, we've shown you the main things you need to pay attention to when starting and maintaining a healthy and loving relationship, as well as how to cope with a relationship that comes to an end.

We've shown you why it's important to love yourself before loving another, and how to prepare for commitment in a relationship.

You saw the importance of the love language, and why setting healthy boundaries actually improves the relationship, as well as why date nights shouldn't be neglected.

We talked about the spiritual and karmic aspects of love and relationships, and how you can stay in God's grace by being a Godly person.

You learned about the importance of intimacy, support and responsibility in a loving relationship, and the ways to move forward and add stability to your love life.

You've read about what men and women want in a relationship, and what kind of labels they put onto each other.

We've shown you the good and bad signs of dealing with conflict, and how to recognize the mind games men play.

Finally, we've talked about what to do and what not to do when your romance is in danger of ending, and how to cope with it once it happens.

Congratulations! Having made it this far means you are now well-prepared to avoid the pitfalls of dating and stay on the right path of creating a healthy, stable relationship.

The only thing that is left is for us to wish you happiness and success on your journey.

Remember, you are loved, valued, and competent.

WHERE TO GO FROM HERE

You can check out the Alise Spiritual Healing & Wellness Center to see how to schedule an intuitive reading, life coaching session, flower essence session, or just to hang out and learn what we are all about. Our website is the following: **www.alisehealingcenter.com**.

Looking for a guest speaker? Please go to our website and invite Alise to speak.

Should you have questions or comments for us, suggestions for future material or tips, feel free to email us at **support@ alisehealingcenter.com**.

CLASS TOURS AND CONFERENCES

Please check our website on upcoming events at www. alisehealingcenter.com.

Also, we have an annual Women's Love of You Conference and you can check up upcoming events at www. loveofyouconference.com

You can also join our mailing list or email us at support@ alisehealingcenter.com.

N♡TES

_____
_____
_____
_____
_____
_____
_____
_____
_____
_____
_____
_____
_____
_____
_____
_____
_____

N♡TES

NOTES

_____
_____
_____
_____
_____
_____
_____
_____
_____
_____
_____
_____
_____
_____
_____
_____
_____
_____

N♡TES

_____

_____

_____

_____

_____

_____

_____

_____

_____

_____

_____

_____

_____

_____

_____

_____

_____

N♡TES

_____
_____
_____
_____
_____
_____
_____
_____
_____
_____
_____
_____
_____
_____
_____
_____
_____
_____

N♡TES

NOTES

N♥TES

NOTES

_____
_____
_____
_____
_____
_____
_____
_____
_____
_____
_____
_____
_____
_____
_____
_____
_____
_____

N♡TES

_____
_____
_____
_____
_____
_____
_____
_____
_____
_____
_____
_____
_____
_____
_____
_____
_____
_____
_____